This Journal Belongs to:

M000031079

Index

Class/Topic	Date	Page

Index

Class/Topic	Date	Page

Index

Class/Topic	Date	Page

Index

Class/Topic	Date	Page

Date/Time: .... Venue: ....

Class Theme:

Mantra/Positive Quote:

Props

- ○ ....
- ○ ....
- ○ ....
- ○ ....
- ○ ....

Oils

- ○ ....
- ○ ....
- ○ ....
- ○ ....
- ○ ....

Music

Sequence:

Post-Class Thoughts & Extra Notes:

Date/Time: .... Venue: ....

Class Theme:

Mantra/Positive Quote:

Props

- ○ ....
- ○ ....
- ○ ....
- ○ ....
- ○ ....

Oils

- ○ ....
- ○ ....
- ○ ....
- ○ ....
- ○ ....

Music

Sequence:

Post-Class Thoughts & Extra Notes:

Date/Time: .... Venue: ....

Class Theme:

Mantra/Positive Quote:

Props
- ○ ....
- ○ ....
- ○ ....
- ○ ....
- ○ ....

Oils
- ○ ....
- ○ ....
- ○ ....
- ○ ....
- ○ ....

Music

Sequence:

Post-Class Thoughts & Extra Notes:

Date/Time: .... Venue: ....

Class Theme:

Mantra/Positive Quote:

Props

- ○ ....
- ○ ....
- ○ ....
- ○ ....
- ○ ....

Oils

- ○ ....
- ○ ....
- ○ ....
- ○ ....
- ○ ....

Music

Sequence:

Post-Class Thoughts & Extra Notes:

Date/Time: .... Venue: ....

Class Theme:

Mantra/Positive Quote:

Props

- ○ ....
- ○ ....
- ○ ....
- ○ ....
- ○ ....

Oils

- ○ ....
- ○ ....
- ○ ....
- ○ ....
- ○ ....

Music

Sequence:

Post-Class Thoughts & Extra Notes:

Date/Time: .... Venue: ....

Class Theme:

Mantra/Positive Quote:

Props

- ○ ....
- ○ ....
- ○ ....
- ○ ....
- ○ ....

Oils

- ○ ....
- ○ ....
- ○ ....
- ○ ....
- ○ ....

Music

Sequence:

Post-Class Thoughts & Extra Notes:

Date/Time: ....   Venue: ....

Class Theme:

Mantra/Positive Quote:

Props	Oils	Music
○	○	
○	○	
○	○	
○	○	
○	○	

Sequence:

Post-Class Thoughts & Extra Notes:

Date/Time: .... Venue: ....

Class Theme:

Mantra/Positive Quote:

Props	Oils	Music
○	○	
○	○	
○	○	
○	○	
○	○	

Sequence:

Post-Class Thoughts & Extra Notes:

Date/Time: .... Venue: ....

Class Theme:

Mantra/Positive Quote:

Props
- ○ ....
- ○ ....
- ○ ....
- ○ ....
- ○ ....

Oils
- ○ ....
- ○ ....
- ○ ....
- ○ ....
- ○ ....

Music

Sequence:

Post-Class Thoughts & Extra Notes:

Date/Time: .... Venue: ....

Class Theme:

Mantra/Positive Quote:

Props

- ○ ....
- ○ ....
- ○ ....
- ○ ....
- ○ ....

Oils

- ○ ....
- ○ ....
- ○ ....
- ○ ....
- ○ ....

Music

Sequence:

Post-Class Thoughts & Extra Notes:

Date/Time: .... Venue: ....

Class Theme:

Mantra/Positive Quote:

Props	Oils	Music
○	○	
○	○	
○	○	
○	○	
○	○	

Sequence:

Post-Class Thoughts & Extra Notes:

Date/Time: .... Venue: ....

Class Theme:

Mantra/Positive Quote:

Props

- ○ ....
- ○ ....
- ○ ....
- ○ ....
- ○ ....

Oils

- ○ ....
- ○ ....
- ○ ....
- ○ ....
- ○ ....

Music

Sequence:

Post-Class Thoughts & Extra Notes:

Date/Time: .... Venue: ....

Class Theme:

Mantra/Positive Quote:

Props

- ○ ....
- ○ ....
- ○ ....
- ○ ....
- ○ ....

Oils

- ○ ....
- ○ ....
- ○ ....
- ○ ....
- ○ ....

Music

Sequence:

Post-Class Thoughts & Extra Notes:

Date/Time: .... Venue: ....

Class Theme:

Mantra/Positive Quote:

Props
- ○ ....
- ○ ....
- ○ ....
- ○ ....
- ○ ....

Oils
- ○ ....
- ○ ....
- ○ ....
- ○ ....
- ○ ....

Music

Sequence:

Post-Class Thoughts & Extra Notes:

Date/Time: .... Venue: ....

Class Theme:

Mantra/Positive Quote:

Props

- ○ ....
- ○ ....
- ○ ....
- ○ ....
- ○ ....

Oils

- ○ ....
- ○ ....
- ○ ....
- ○ ....
- ○ ....

Music

Sequence:

Post-Class Thoughts & Extra Notes:

Date/Time: .... Venue: ....

Class Theme:

Mantra/Positive Quote:

Props	Oils	Music
○ _____	○ _____	
○ _____	○ _____	
○ _____	○ _____	
○ _____	○ _____	
○ _____	○ _____	

Sequence:

Post-Class Thoughts & Extra Notes:

Class Theme:

Mantra/Positive Quote:

Props

- ○ ....
- ○ ....
- ○ ....
- ○ ....
- ○ ....

Oils

- ○ ....
- ○ ....
- ○ ....
- ○ ....
- ○ ....

Music

Sequence:

Post-Class Thoughts & Extra Notes:

Date/Time: .... Venue: ....

Class Theme:

Mantra/Positive Quote:

Props	Oils	Music
○ _____	○ _____	
○ _____	○ _____	
○ _____	○ _____	
○ _____	○ _____	
○ _____	○ _____	

Sequence:

Post-Class Thoughts & Extra Notes:

Date/Time: .... Venue: ....

Class Theme:

Mantra/Positive Quote:

Props
- ○ ....
- ○ ....
- ○ ....
- ○ ....
- ○ ....

Oils
- ○ ....
- ○ ....
- ○ ....
- ○ ....
- ○ ....

Music

Sequence:

Post-Class Thoughts & Extra Notes:

Date/Time: .... Venue: ....

Class Theme:

Mantra/Positive Quote:

Props	Oils	Music
○ _____	○ _____	
○ _____	○ _____	
○ _____	○ _____	
○ _____	○ _____	
○ _____	○ _____	

Sequence:

Post-Class Thoughts & Extra Notes:

Date/Time: .... Venue: ....

Class Theme:

Mantra/Positive Quote:

Props

- ○ ....
- ○ ....
- ○ ....
- ○ ....
- ○ ....

Oils

- ○ ....
- ○ ....
- ○ ....
- ○ ....
- ○ ....

Music

Sequence:

Post-Class Thoughts & Extra Notes:

Date/Time: .... Venue: ....

Class Theme:

Mantra/Positive Quote:

Props
- ○ ....
- ○ ....
- ○ ....
- ○ ....
- ○ ....

Oils
- ○ ....
- ○ ....
- ○ ....
- ○ ....
- ○ ....

Music

Sequence:

Post-Class Thoughts & Extra Notes:

Date/Time: .... Venue: ....

Class Theme:

Mantra/Positive Quote:

Props	Oils	Music
○ _____	○ _____	
○ _____	○ _____	
○ _____	○ _____	
○ _____	○ _____	
○ _____	○ _____	

Sequence:

Post-Class Thoughts & Extra Notes:

Date/Time: .... Venue: ....

Class Theme:

Mantra/Positive Quote:

Props

- ○ ....
- ○ ....
- ○ ....
- ○ ....
- ○ ....

Oils

- ○ ....
- ○ ....
- ○ ....
- ○ ....
- ○ ....

Music

Sequence:

Post-Class Thoughts & Extra Notes:

Date/Time: .... Venue: ....

Class Theme:

Mantra/Positive Quote:

Props	Oils	Music
○	○	
○	○	
○	○	
○	○	
○	○	

Sequence:

Post-Class Thoughts & Extra Notes:

Date/Time: .... Venue: ....

Class Theme:

Mantra/Positive Quote:

Props	Oils	Music
○	○	
○	○	
○	○	
○	○	
○	○	

Sequence:

Post-Class Thoughts & Extra Notes:

Date/Time: .... Venue: ....

Class Theme: Mantra/Positive Quote:

Props
- ◯ ....
- ◯ ....
- ◯ ....
- ◯ ....
- ◯ ....

Oils
- ◯ ....
- ◯ ....
- ◯ ....
- ◯ ....
- ◯ ....

Music

Sequence:

Post-Class Thoughts & Extra Notes:

Date/Time: .... Venue: ....

Class Theme:

Mantra/Positive Quote:

Props
- ○ ....
- ○ ....
- ○ ....
- ○ ....
- ○ ....

Oils
- ○ ....
- ○ ....
- ○ ....
- ○ ....
- ○ ....

Music

Sequence:

Post-Class Thoughts & Extra Notes:

Date/Time: .... Venue: ....

Class Theme:

Mantra/Positive Quote:

Props	Oils	Music
○	○	
○	○	
○	○	
○	○	
○	○	

Sequence:

Post-Class Thoughts & Extra Notes:

Date/Time: .... Venue: ....

Class Theme:

Mantra/Positive Quote:

Props

- ○ ....
- ○ ....
- ○ ....
- ○ ....
- ○ ....

Oils

- ○ ....
- ○ ....
- ○ ....
- ○ ....
- ○ ....

Music

Sequence:

Post-Class Thoughts & Extra Notes:

Date/Time: .... Venue: ....

Class Theme:

Mantra/Positive Quote:

Props

- ○ ....
- ○ ....
- ○ ....
- ○ ....
- ○ ....

Oils

- ○ ....
- ○ ....
- ○ ....
- ○ ....
- ○ ....

Music

Sequence:

Post-Class Thoughts & Extra Notes:

Date/Time: .... Venue: ....

Class Theme:

Mantra/Positive Quote:

Props	Oils	Music
○	○	
○	○	
○	○	
○	○	
○	○	

Sequence:

Post-Class Thoughts & Extra Notes:

Date/Time: .... Venue: ....

Class Theme:

Mantra/Positive Quote:

Props	Oils	Music
○	○	
○	○	
○	○	
○	○	
○	○	

Sequence:

Post-Class Thoughts & Extra Notes:

Date/Time: .... Venue: ....

Class Theme:

Mantra/Positive Quote:

Props	Oils	Music
○	○	
○	○	
○	○	
○	○	
○	○	

Sequence:

Post-Class Thoughts & Extra Notes:

Date/Time: .... Venue: ....

Class Theme:

Mantra/Positive Quote:

Props	Oils	Music
○	○	
○	○	
○	○	
○	○	
○	○	

Sequence:

Post-Class Thoughts & Extra Notes:

Date/Time: .... Venue: ....

Class Theme:

Mantra/Positive Quote:

Props

- ○ ....
- ○ ....
- ○ ....
- ○ ....
- ○ ....

Oils

- ○ ....
- ○ ....
- ○ ....
- ○ ....
- ○ ....

Music

Sequence:

Post-Class Thoughts & Extra Notes:

Date/Time: .... Venue: ....

Class Theme:

Mantra/Positive Quote:

Props

- ○ _____
- ○ _____
- ○ _____
- ○ _____
- ○ _____

Oils

- ○ _____
- ○ _____
- ○ _____
- ○ _____
- ○ _____

Music

Sequence:

Post-Class Thoughts & Extra Notes:

Date/Time: ....   Venue: ....

Class Theme:

Mantra/Positive Quote:

Props	Oils	Music
○	○	
○	○	
○	○	
○	○	
○	○	

Sequence:

Post-Class Thoughts & Extra Notes:

Date/Time: .... Venue: ....

Class Theme:

Mantra/Positive Quote:

Props	Oils	Music
○	○	
○	○	
○	○	
○	○	
○	○	

Sequence:

Post-Class Thoughts & Extra Notes:

Date/Time: .... Venue: ....

Class Theme:

Mantra/Positive Quote:

Props

- ○ ....
- ○ ....
- ○ ....
- ○ ....
- ○ ....

Oils

- ○ ....
- ○ ....
- ○ ....
- ○ ....
- ○ ....

Music

Sequence:

Post-Class Thoughts & Extra Notes:

Date/Time: .... Venue: ....

Class Theme:

Mantra/Positive Quote:

Props	Oils	Music
○	○	
○	○	
○	○	
○	○	
○	○	

Sequence:

Post-Class Thoughts & Extra Notes:

Date/Time: .... Venue: ....

Class Theme:

Mantra/Positive Quote:

Props
- ○ ....
- ○ ....
- ○ ....
- ○ ....
- ○ ....

Oils
- ○ ....
- ○ ....
- ○ ....
- ○ ....
- ○ ....

Music

Sequence:

Post-Class Thoughts & Extra Notes:

Date/Time: .... Venue: ....

Class Theme:

Mantra/Positive Quote:

Props

- ○ ....
- ○ ....
- ○ ....
- ○ ....
- ○ ....

Oils

- ○ ....
- ○ ....
- ○ ....
- ○ ....
- ○ ....

Music

Sequence:

Post-Class Thoughts & Extra Notes:

Date/Time: .... Venue: ....

Class Theme:

Mantra/Positive Quote:

Props
- ○ ....
- ○ ....
- ○ ....
- ○ ....
- ○ ....

Oils
- ○ ....
- ○ ....
- ○ ....
- ○ ....
- ○ ....

Music

Sequence:

Post-Class Thoughts & Extra Notes:

Date/Time: .... Venue: ....

Class Theme:

Mantra/Positive Quote:

Props	Oils	Music
○	○	
○	○	
○	○	
○	○	
○	○	

Sequence:

Post-Class Thoughts & Extra Notes:

Date/Time: .... Venue: ....

Class Theme:

Mantra/Positive Quote:

Props

- ○ ....
- ○ ....
- ○ ....
- ○ ....
- ○ ....

Oils

- ○ ....
- ○ ....
- ○ ....
- ○ ....
- ○ ....

Music

Sequence:

Post-Class Thoughts & Extra Notes:

Date/Time: .... Venue: ....

Class Theme:

Mantra/Positive Quote:

Props	Oils	Music
○	○	
○	○	
○	○	
○	○	
○	○	

Sequence:

Post-Class Thoughts & Extra Notes:

Date/Time: .... Venue: ....

Class Theme:

Mantra/Positive Quote:

Props	Oils	Music
○	○	
○	○	
○	○	
○	○	
○	○	

Sequence:

Post-Class Thoughts & Extra Notes:

Date/Time: .... Venue: ....

Class Theme:

Mantra/Positive Quote:

Props

- ○ ....
- ○ ....
- ○ ....
- ○ ....
- ○ ....

Oils

- ○ ....
- ○ ....
- ○ ....
- ○ ....
- ○ ....

Music

Sequence:

Post-Class Thoughts & Extra Notes:

Date/Time: .... Venue: ....

Class Theme:

Mantra/Positive Quote:

Props	Oils	Music
○	○	
○	○	
○	○	
○	○	
○	○	

Sequence:

Post-Class Thoughts & Extra Notes:

Date/Time: .... Venue: ....

Class Theme:

Mantra/Positive Quote:

Props	Oils	Music
○	○	
○	○	
○	○	
○	○	
○	○	

Sequence:

Post-Class Thoughts & Extra Notes:

Date/Time: .... Venue: ....

Class Theme:

Mantra/Positive Quote:

Props
- ○ ....
- ○ ....
- ○ ....
- ○ ....
- ○ ....

Oils
- ○ ....
- ○ ....
- ○ ....
- ○ ....
- ○ ....

Music

Sequence:

Post-Class Thoughts & Extra Notes:

Date/Time: .... Venue: ....

Class Theme:

Mantra/Positive Quote:

Props	Oils	Music
○	○	
○	○	
○	○	
○	○	
○	○	

Sequence:

Post-Class Thoughts & Extra Notes:

Date/Time: .... Venue: ....

Class Theme:

Mantra/Positive Quote:

Props	Oils	Music
○	○	
○	○	
○	○	
○	○	
○	○	

Sequence:

Post-Class Thoughts & Extra Notes:

Date/Time: .... Venue: ....

Class Theme:

Mantra/Positive Quote:

Props

- ○ ....
- ○ ....
- ○ ....
- ○ ....
- ○ ....

Oils

- ○ ....
- ○ ....
- ○ ....
- ○ ....
- ○ ....

Music

Sequence:

Post-Class Thoughts & Extra Notes:

Date/Time: .... Venue: ....

Class Theme:

Mantra/Positive Quote:

Props

- ○ ....
- ○ ....
- ○ ....
- ○ ....
- ○ ....

Oils

- ○ ....
- ○ ....
- ○ ....
- ○ ....
- ○ ....

Music

Sequence:

Post-Class Thoughts & Extra Notes:

Date/Time: .... Venue: ....

Class Theme:

Mantra/Positive Quote:

Props	Oils	Music
○	○	
○	○	
○	○	
○	○	
○	○	

Sequence:

Post-Class Thoughts & Extra Notes:

Date/Time: .... Venue: ....

Class Theme:

Mantra/Positive Quote:

Props	Oils	Music
○	○	
○	○	
○	○	
○	○	
○	○	

Sequence:

Post-Class Thoughts & Extra Notes:

Date/Time: .... Venue: ....

Class Theme:

Mantra/Positive Quote:

Props	Oils	Music
○	○	
○	○	
○	○	
○	○	
○	○	

Sequence:

Post-Class Thoughts & Extra Notes:

Date/Time: .... Venue: ....

Class Theme:

Mantra/Positive Quote:

Props	Oils	Music
○	○	
○	○	
○	○	
○	○	
○	○	

Sequence:

Post-Class Thoughts & Extra Notes:

Date/Time: .... Venue: ....

Class Theme:

Mantra/Positive Quote:

Props

- ○ ....
- ○ ....
- ○ ....
- ○ ....
- ○ ....

Oils

- ○ ....
- ○ ....
- ○ ....
- ○ ....
- ○ ....

Music

Sequence:

Post-Class Thoughts & Extra Notes:

Date/Time: .... Venue: ....

Class Theme:

Mantra/Positive Quote:

Props	Oils	Music
○	○	
○	○	
○	○	
○	○	
○	○	

Sequence:

Post-Class Thoughts & Extra Notes:

Date/Time: .... Venue: ....

Class Theme:

Mantra/Positive Quote:

Props

- ○ ....
- ○ ....
- ○ ....
- ○ ....
- ○ ....

Oils

- ○ ....
- ○ ....
- ○ ....
- ○ ....
- ○ ....

Music

Sequence:

Post-Class Thoughts & Extra Notes:

Date/Time: .... Venue: ....

Class Theme:

Mantra/Positive Quote:

Props

○ ....
○ ....
○ ....
○ ....
○ ....

Oils

○ ....
○ ....
○ ....
○ ....
○ ....

Music

Sequence:

Post-Class Thoughts & Extra Notes:

Date/Time: .... Venue: ....

Class Theme:

Mantra/Positive Quote:

Props	Oils	Music
○ _____	○ _____	
○ _____	○ _____	
○ _____	○ _____	
○ _____	○ _____	
○ _____	○ _____	

Sequence:

Post-Class Thoughts & Extra Notes:

Date/Time: .... Venue: ....

Class Theme:

Mantra/Positive Quote:

Props	Oils	Music
○	○	
○	○	
○	○	
○	○	
○	○	

Sequence:

Post-Class Thoughts & Extra Notes:

Date/Time: .... Venue: ....

Class Theme:

Mantra/Positive Quote:

Props
- ○ ....
- ○ ....
- ○ ....
- ○ ....
- ○ ....

Oils
- ○ ....
- ○ ....
- ○ ....
- ○ ....
- ○ ....

Music

Sequence:

Post-Class Thoughts & Extra Notes:

Date/Time: .... Venue: ....

Class Theme:

Mantra/Positive Quote:

Props
- ○ ....
- ○ ....
- ○ ....
- ○ ....
- ○ ....

Oils
- ○ ....
- ○ ....
- ○ ....
- ○ ....
- ○ ....

Music

Sequence:

Post-Class Thoughts & Extra Notes:

Date/Time: ....   Venue: ....

Class Theme:

Mantra/Positive Quote:

Props	Oils	Music
○	○	
○	○	
○	○	
○	○	
○	○	

Sequence:

Post-Class Thoughts & Extra Notes:

Date/Time: .... Venue: ....

Class Theme:

Mantra/Positive Quote:

Props

- ○ ....
- ○ ....
- ○ ....
- ○ ....
- ○ ....

Oils

- ○ ....
- ○ ....
- ○ ....
- ○ ....
- ○ ....

Music

Sequence:

Post-Class Thoughts & Extra Notes:

Date/Time: .... Venue: ....

Class Theme: Mantra/Positive Quote:

Props
- ○ ....
- ○ ....
- ○ ....
- ○ ....
- ○ ....

Oils
- ○ ....
- ○ ....
- ○ ....
- ○ ....
- ○ ....

Music

Sequence:

Post-Class Thoughts & Extra Notes:

Date/Time: .... Venue: ....

Class Theme:

Mantra/Positive Quote:

Props	Oils	Music
○ _____	○ _____	
○ _____	○ _____	
○ _____	○ _____	
○ _____	○ _____	
○ _____	○ _____	

Sequence:

Post-Class Thoughts & Extra Notes:

Date/Time: .... Venue: ....

Class Theme:

Mantra/Positive Quote:

Props

- ○ ....
- ○ ....
- ○ ....
- ○ ....
- ○ ....

Oils

- ○ ....
- ○ ....
- ○ ....
- ○ ....
- ○ ....

Music

Sequence:

Post-Class Thoughts & Extra Notes:

Date/Time: .... Venue: ....

Class Theme:

Mantra/Positive Quote:

Props	Oils	Music
○ _____	○ _____	
○ _____	○ _____	
○ _____	○ _____	
○ _____	○ _____	
○ _____	○ _____	

Sequence:

Post-Class Thoughts & Extra Notes:

Date/Time: .... Venue: ....

Class Theme:

Mantra/Positive Quote:

Props	Oils	Music
○	○	
○	○	
○	○	
○	○	
○	○	

Sequence:

Post-Class Thoughts & Extra Notes:

Date/Time: .... Venue: ....

Class Theme:

Mantra/Positive Quote:

Props
- ○ ....
- ○ ....
- ○ ....
- ○ ....
- ○ ....

Oils
- ○ ....
- ○ ....
- ○ ....
- ○ ....
- ○ ....

Music

Sequence:

Post-Class Thoughts & Extra Notes:

Date/Time: .... Venue: ....

Class Theme:

Mantra/Positive Quote:

Props

- ○ ....
- ○ ....
- ○ ....
- ○ ....
- ○ ....

Oils

- ○ ....
- ○ ....
- ○ ....
- ○ ....
- ○ ....

Music

Sequence:

Post-Class Thoughts & Extra Notes:

Date/Time: .... Venue: ....

Class Theme:

Mantra/Positive Quote:

Props	Oils	Music
○	○	
○	○	
○	○	
○	○	
○	○	

Sequence:

Post-Class Thoughts & Extra Notes:

Class Theme:

Mantra/Positive Quote:

Props
○ ....
○ ....
○ ....
○ ....
○ ....

Oils
○ ....
○ ....
○ ....
○ ....
○ ....

Music

Sequence:

Post-Class Thoughts & Extra Notes:

Date/Time: .... Venue: ....

Class Theme:

Mantra/Positive Quote:

Props	Oils	Music
○	○	
○	○	
○	○	
○	○	
○	○	

Sequence:

Post-Class Thoughts & Extra Notes:

Date/Time: .... Venue: ....

Class Theme:

Mantra/Positive Quote:

Props	Oils	Music
○ _____	○ _____	
○ _____	○ _____	
○ _____	○ _____	
○ _____	○ _____	
○ _____	○ _____	

Sequence:

Post-Class Thoughts & Extra Notes:

Date/Time: .... Venue: ....

Class Theme:

Mantra/Positive Quote:

Props	Oils	Music
○	○	
○	○	
○	○	
○	○	
○	○	

Sequence:

Post-Class Thoughts & Extra Notes:

Date/Time: .... Venue: ....

Class Theme:

Mantra/Positive Quote:

Props

- ○ ....
- ○ ....
- ○ ....
- ○ ....
- ○ ....

Oils

- ○ ....
- ○ ....
- ○ ....
- ○ ....
- ○ ....

Music

Sequence:

Post-Class Thoughts & Extra Notes:

Date/Time: .... Venue: ....

Class Theme:

Mantra/Positive Quote:

Props	Oils	Music
○	○	
○	○	
○	○	
○	○	
○	○	

Sequence:

Post-Class Thoughts & Extra Notes:

Date/Time: .... Venue: ....

Class Theme:

Mantra/Positive Quote:

Props	Oils	Music
○ _____	○ _____	
○ _____	○ _____	
○ _____	○ _____	
○ _____	○ _____	
○ _____	○ _____	

Sequence:

Post-Class Thoughts & Extra Notes:

Date/Time: .... Venue: ....

Class Theme:

Mantra/Positive Quote:

Props
- ○ ....
- ○ ....
- ○ ....
- ○ ....
- ○ ....

Oils
- ○ ....
- ○ ....
- ○ ....
- ○ ....
- ○ ....

Music

Sequence:

Post-Class Thoughts & Extra Notes:

Date/Time: .... Venue: ....

Class Theme:

Mantra/Positive Quote:

Props

- ○ _____
- ○ _____
- ○ _____
- ○ _____
- ○ _____

Oils

- ○ _____
- ○ _____
- ○ _____
- ○ _____
- ○ _____

Music

Sequence:

Post-Class Thoughts & Extra Notes:

Made in the USA
Middletown, DE
08 October 2021

49898919R00102